SECOND BOOK

of

PRACTICAL STUDIES

for

FRENCH HORN

by

ROBERT W. GETCHELL

Foreword

The SECOND BOOK OF PRACTICAL STUDIES is designed to logically extend the techniques already presented in the FIRST BOOK and also to introduce and develop new techniques and rhythms that will offer a challenge to the intermediate student. Through the use of slightly more difficult and more extended studies, it is hoped that the material included in this book may more fully develop general musicianship and more feeling for style and interpretation and thus act as a foundation for solo literature.

The following rhythms are introduced and developed in this Second Book:

3

4

73

74

75

76

77

78

79

80

81

82

83

84

Scherzando

85

Alla Minuet

86

87

88

89

Largo espressivo

90

Leggiero

91

92

93

94

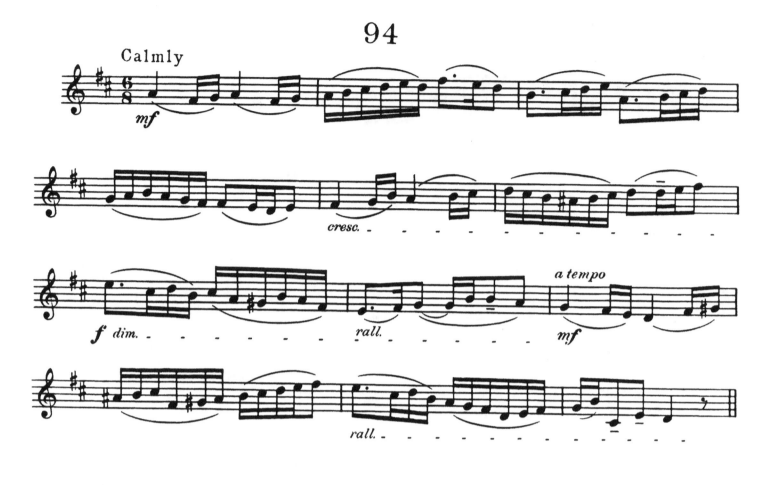

95

96

97

98

99

100

101

102

104

105

106

107

108

109

110

111

(Utilizing the nine major keys covered in Books I & II)

TO THE STUDENT: The care with which a player conditions his lip prior to a rehearsal or a practice session plays a very important part in determining how successfully his embouchure will respond   A thorough "warm-up" routine is especially important before the *initial* practice session each day

Intonation, tone quality, range, and endurance are all affected by a careful warm-up which has the effect of flexing the lip muscles and preparing them for the day's work

Following are some suggested warm up exercises   Supplement these either with exercises of your own or from some of the fine books which are written for this purpose. Remember to rest frequently, if even for short periods of time.

LONG TONES - Rest briefly after each long tone.

(Continue in descending half-steps.)

(Continue in descending half-steps.)